CHURCH: _____
_____

EMAIL: _____

PHONE: _____

ADDRESS: _____
_____

Start Date:	End Date:	#:

IF FOUND, PLEASE CONTACT OR

APPLICATION FOR CHURCH MEMBERSHIP FORM

PERSONAL INFORMATION

First name:	Middle:	Last:	Birthdate:

Address:	City:

State:	ZIP:	Email:

Phone:	Home phone:	Identity Number:

Tick Appropriate Box ☐ Single ☐ Married ☐ Divorced ☐ Widowed ☐ Separated ☐ Minor

Have you been baptized ? Yes ☐   No ☐   Baptism Date: Baptism Location:

Have you been confirmed?   Yes ☐   No ☐   Confirmation date: Confirmation place:

Sex ☐ Male ☐ Female   Employer:

Work Address:	City:	State:	ZIP:

If student, Name of school:	City:	State:

Spouse/Parent's Name:	Employer:	Work Phone:

Emergency contact:	Phone:

PARENT/GUARDIAN/SPOUSE INFORMATION

Name:	Relationship:

Address:	City:	State:	Phone:

E-Mail:	Birthdate:	SSN:

Employer:	Address:

Work Phone: This person is currently a member here? (Circle appropriate)   Yes   No

CHILDREN (IF APPLICABLE)

Name:	Age	Contact

About your household (What would you like the church to know about your family)

_____

_____

_____

_____

_____

_____   _____

Date   Signature

APPLICATION FOR CHURCH MEMBERSHIP FORM

PERSONAL INFORMATION

First name:	Middle:	Last:	Birthdate:

Address:	City:

State:	ZIP:	Email:

Phone:	Home phone:	Identity Number:

Tick Appropriate Box ☐ Single ☐ Married ☐ Divorced ☐ Widowed ☐ Separated ☐ Minor

Have you been baptized ? Yes ☐ No ☐ Baptism Date: Baptism Location:

Have you been confirmed? Yes ☐ No ☐ Confirmation date: Confirmation place:

Sex ☐ Male ☐ Female Employer:

Work Address:	City:	State:	ZIP:

If student, Name of school:	City:	State:

Spouse/Parent's Name:	Employer:	Work Phone:

Emergency contact:	Phone:

PARENT/GUARDIAN/SPOUSE INFORMATION

Name:	Relationship:

Address:	City:	State:	Phone:

E-Mail:	Birthdate:	SSN:

Employer:	Address:

Work Phone: This person is currently a member here? (Circle appropriate)   Yes   No

CHILDREN (IF APPLICABLE)

Name:	Age	Contact

About your household (What would you like the church to know about your family)

_____

_____

_____

_____

_____

_____

_____	_____
Date	Signature

APPLICATION FOR CHURCH MEMBERSHIP FORM

PERSONAL INFORMATION

First name:	Middle:	Last:	Birthdate:

Address: | City:

State: | ZIP: | Email:

Phone: | Home phone: | Identity Number:

Tick Appropriate Box ☐ Single ☐ Married ☐ Divorced ☐ Widowed ☐ Separated ☐ Minor

Have you been baptized ? Yes ☐ No ☐ Baptism Date: | Baptism Location:

Have you been confirmed? Yes ☐ No ☐ Confirmation date: | Confirmation place:

Sex ☐ Male ☐ Female | Employer:

Work Address: | City: | State: | ZIP:

If student, Name of school: | City: | State:

Spouse/Parent's Name: | Employer: | Work Phone:

Emergency contact: | Phone:

PARENT/GUARDIAN/SPOUSE INFORMATION

Name: | Relationship:

Address: | City: | State: | Phone:

E-Mail: | Birthdate: | SSN:

Employer: | Address:

Work Phone: | This person is currently a member here? (Circle appropriate) Yes No

CHILDREN (IF APPLICABLE)

Name:	Age	Contact

About your household (What would you like the church to know about your family)

_____

_____

_____

_____

_____

Date | Signature

APPLICATION FOR CHURCH MEMBERSHIP FORM

PERSONAL INFORMATION

First name:	Middle:	Last:	Birthdate:

Address:	City:

State:	ZIP:	Email:

Phone:	Home phone:	Identity Number:

Tick Appropriate Box ☐ Single ☐ Married ☐ Divorced ☐ Widowed ☐ Separated ☐ Minor

Have you been baptized ? Yes ☐ No ☐	Baptism Date:	Baptism Location:

Have you been confirmed? Yes ☐ No ☐	Confirmation date:	Confirmation place:

Sex ☐ Male ☐ Female	Employer:

Work Address:	City:	State:	ZIP:

If student, Name of school:	City:	State:

Spouse/Parent's Name:	Employer:	Work Phone:

Emergency contact:	Phone:

PARENT/GUARDIAN/SPOUSE INFORMATION

Name:	Relationship:

Address:	City:	State:	Phone:

E-Mail:	Birthdate:	SSN:

Employer:	Address:

Work Phone:	This person is currently a member here? (Circle appropriate) Yes No

CHILDREN (IF APPLICABLE)

Name:	Age	Contact

About your household (What would you like the church to know about your family)

_____

_____

_____

_____

_____

_____	_____
Date	Signature

APPLICATION FOR CHURCH MEMBERSHIP FORM

PERSONAL INFORMATION

First name:	Middle:	Last:	Birthdate:

Address:	City:

State:	ZIP:	Email:

Phone:	Home phone:	Identity Number:

Tick Appropriate Box ☐ Single ☐ Married ☐ Divorced ☐ Widowed ☐ Separated ☐ Minor

Have you been baptized ? Yes ☐ No ☐	Baptism Date:	Baptism Location:

Have you been confirmed? Yes ☐ No ☐	Confirmation date:	Confirmation place:

Sex ☐ Male ☐ Female	Employer:

Work Address:	City:	State:	ZIP:

If student, Name of school:	City:	State:

Spouse/Parent's Name:	Employer:	Work Phone:

Emergency contact:	Phone:

PARENT/GUARDIAN/SPOUSE INFORMATION

Name:	Relationship:

Address:	City:	State:	Phone:

E-Mail:	Birthdate:	SSN:

Employer:	Address:

Work Phone:	This person is currently a member here? (Circle appropriate) Yes No

CHILDREN (IF APPLICABLE)

Name:	Age	Contact

About your household (What would you like the church to know about your family)

_____

_____

_____

_____

_____

Date   Signature

APPLICATION FOR CHURCH MEMBERSHIP FORM

PERSONAL INFORMATION

First name:	Middle:	Last:	Birthdate:

Address:	City:

State:	ZIP:	Email:

Phone:	Home phone:	Identity Number:

Tick Appropriate Box ☐ Single ☐ Married ☐ Divorced ☐ Widowed ☐ Separated ☐ Minor

Have you been baptized ?   Yes ☐   No ☐   Baptism Date: Baptism Location:

Have you been confirmed?   Yes ☐   No ☐   Confirmation date: Confirmation place:

Sex ☐ Male ☐ Female   Employer:

Work Address:	City:	State:	ZIP:

If student, Name of school: City: State:

Spouse/Parent's Name:	Employer:	Work Phone:

Emergency contact:	Phone:

PARENT/GUARDIAN/SPOUSE INFORMATION

Name:	Relationship:

Address:	City:	State:	Phone:

E-Mail:	Birthdate:	SSN:

Employer:	Address:

Work Phone: This person is currently a member here? (Circle appropriate)   Yes   No

CHILDREN (IF APPLICABLE)

Name:	Age	Contact

About your household (What would you like the church to know about your family)

_____

_____

_____

_____

_____

_____	_____
Date	Signature

APPLICATION FOR CHURCH MEMBERSHIP FORM

PERSONAL INFORMATION

First name:	Middle:	Last:	Birthdate:

Address:	City:

State:	ZIP:	Email:

Phone:	Home phone:	Identity Number:

Tick Appropriate Box ☐ Single ☐ Married ☐ Divorced ☐ Widowed ☐ Separated ☐ Minor

Have you been baptized ? Yes ☐ No ☐   Baptism Date: Baptism Location:

Have you been confirmed? Yes ☐ No ☐   Confirmation date: Confirmation place:

Sex ☐ Male ☐ Female   Employer:

Work Address:	City:	State:	ZIP:

If student, Name of school:	City:	State:

Spouse/Parent's Name:	Employer:	Work Phone:

Emergency contact:	Phone:

PARENT/GUARDIAN/SPOUSE INFORMATION

Name:	Relationship:

Address:	City:	State:	Phone:

E-Mail:	Birthdate:	SSN:

Employer:	Address:

Work Phone: This person is currently a member here? (Circle appropriate)   Yes   No

CHILDREN (IF APPLICABLE)

Name:	Age	Contact

About your household (What would you like the church to know about your family)

_____

_____

_____

_____

_____

_____	_____
Date	Signature

APPLICATION FOR CHURCH MEMBERSHIP FORM

PERSONAL INFORMATION

First name:	Middle:	Last:	Birthdate:

Address: | City:

State: | ZIP: | Email:

Phone: | Home phone: | Identity Number:

Tick Appropriate Box ☐ Single ☐ Married ☐ Divorced ☐ Widowed ☐ Separated ☐ Minor

Have you been baptized ?　Yes ☐　　No ☐　　Baptism Date: | Baptism Location:

Have you been confirmed?　Yes ☐　　No ☐　　Confirmation date: | Confirmation place:

Sex ☐ Male ☐ Female | Employer:

Work Address: | City: | State: | ZIP:

If student, Name of school: | City: | State:

Spouse/Parent's Name: | Employer: | Work Phone:

Emergency contact: | Phone:

PARENT/GUARDIAN/SPOUSE INFORMATION

Name: | Relationship:

Address: | City: | State: | Phone:

E-Mail: | Birthdate: | SSN:

Employer: | Address:

Work Phone: | This person is currently a member here? (Circle appropriate)　　Yes　　No

CHILDREN (IF APPLICABLE)

Name:	Age	Contact

About your household (What would you like the church to know about your family)

_____

_____

_____

_____

_____

_____　　　　_____

Date　　　　　　　　　　　　　　　　Signature

APPLICATION FOR CHURCH MEMBERSHIP FORM

PERSONAL INFORMATION

First name:	Middle:	Last:	Birthdate:

Address:	City:

State:	ZIP:	Email:

Phone:	Home phone:	Identity Number:

Tick Appropriate Box ☐ Single ☐ Married ☐ Divorced ☐ Widowed ☐ Separated ☐ Minor

Have you been baptized ? Yes ☐ No ☐ Baptism Date:	Baptism Location:

Have you been confirmed? Yes ☐ No ☐ Confirmation date:	Confirmation place:

Sex ☐ Male ☐ Female	Employer:

Work Address:	City:	State:	ZIP:

If student, Name of school:	City:	State:

Spouse/Parent's Name:	Employer:	Work Phone:

Emergency contact:	Phone:

PARENT/GUARDIAN/SPOUSE INFORMATION

Name:	Relationship:

Address:	City:	State:	Phone:

E-Mail:	Birthdate:	SSN:

Employer:	Address:

Work Phone: This person is currently a member here? (Circle appropriate)   Yes   No

CHILDREN (IF APPLICABLE)

Name:	Age	Contact

About your household (What would you like the church to know about your family)

_____

_____

_____

_____

_____

Date	Signature

APPLICATION FOR CHURCH MEMBERSHIP FORM

PERSONAL INFORMATION

First name:	Middle:	Last:	Birthdate:

Address: | City:

State: | ZIP: | Email:

Phone: | Home phone: | Identity Number:

Tick Appropriate Box ☐ Single ☐ Married ☐ Divorced ☐ Widowed ☐ Separated ☐ Minor

Have you been baptized ? Yes ☐ No ☐ Baptism Date: | Baptism Location:

Have you been confirmed? Yes ☐ No ☐ Confirmation date: | Confirmation place:

Sex ☐ Male ☐ Female | Employer:

Work Address: | City: | State: | ZIP:

If student, Name of school: | City: | State:

Spouse/Parent's Name: | Employer: | Work Phone:

Emergency contact: | Phone:

PARENT/GUARDIAN/SPOUSE INFORMATION

Name: | Relationship:

Address: | City: | State: | Phone:

E-Mail: | Birthdate: | SSN:

Employer: | Address:

Work Phone: | This person is currently a member here? (Circle appropriate)   Yes   No

CHILDREN (IF APPLICABLE)

Name:	Age	Contact

About your household (What would you like the church to know about your family)

_____

_____

_____

_____

_____

_____

_____   _____

Date   Signature

APPLICATION FOR CHURCH MEMBERSHIP FORM

PERSONAL INFORMATION

First name:	Middle:	Last:	Birthdate:

Address:	City:

State:	ZIP:	Email:

Phone:	Home phone:	Identity Number:

Tick Appropriate Box ☐ Single ☐ Married ☐ Divorced ☐ Widowed ☐ Separated ☐ Minor

Have you been baptized ? Yes ☐   No ☐   Baptism Date: Baptism Location:

Have you been confirmed?   Yes ☐   No ☐   Confirmation date: Confirmation place:

Sex ☐ Male ☐ Female   Employer:

Work Address:	City:	State:	ZIP:

If student, Name of school: City: State:

Spouse/Parent's Name:	Employer:	Work Phone:

Emergency contact:	Phone:

PARENT/GUARDIAN/SPOUSE INFORMATION

Name:	Relationship:

Address:	City:	State:	Phone:

E-Mail:	Birthdate:	SSN:

Employer:	Address:

Work Phone:	This person is currently a member here? (Circle appropriate) Yes No

CHILDREN (IF APPLICABLE)

Name:	Age	Contact

About your household (What would you like the church to know about your family)

_____

_____

_____

_____

_____

_____	_____
Date	Signature

APPLICATION FOR CHURCH MEMBERSHIP FORM

PERSONAL INFORMATION

First name:	Middle:	Last:	Birthdate:

Address:	City:

State:	ZIP:	Email:

Phone:	Home phone:	Identity Number:

Tick Appropriate Box ☐ Single ☐ Married ☐ Divorced ☐ Widowed ☐ Separated ☐ Minor

Have you been baptized ? Yes ☐ No ☐	Baptism Date:	Baptism Location:

Have you been confirmed? Yes ☐ No ☐	Confirmation date:	Confirmation place:

Sex ☐ Male ☐ Female	Employer:

Work Address:	City:	State:	ZIP:

If student, Name of school:	City:	State:

Spouse/Parent's Name:	Employer:	Work Phone:

Emergency contact:	Phone:

PARENT/GUARDIAN/SPOUSE INFORMATION

Name:	Relationship:

Address:	City:	State:	Phone:

E-Mail:	Birthdate:	SSN:

Employer:	Address:

Work Phone:	This person is currently a member here? (Circle appropriate)	Yes No

CHILDREN (IF APPLICABLE)

Name:	Age	Contact

About your household (What would you like the church to know about your family)

_____

_____

_____

_____

_____

Date	Signature

APPLICATION FOR CHURCH MEMBERSHIP FORM

PERSONAL INFORMATION

First name:	Middle:	Last:	Birthdate:

Address:	City:

State:	ZIP:	Email:

Phone:	Home phone:	Identity Number:

Tick Appropriate Box ☐ Single ☐ Married ☐ Divorced ☐ Widowed ☐ Separated ☐ Minor

Have you been baptized ? Yes ☐ No ☐ Baptism Date: Baptism Location:

Have you been confirmed? Yes ☐ No ☐ Confirmation date: Confirmation place:

Sex ☐ Male ☐ Female Employer:

Work Address:	City:	State:	ZIP:

If student, Name of school: City: State:

Spouse/Parent's Name:	Employer:	Work Phone:

Emergency contact:	Phone:

PARENT/GUARDIAN/SPOUSE INFORMATION

Name:	Relationship:

Address:	City:	State:	Phone:

E-Mail:	Birthdate:	SSN:

Employer:	Address:

Work Phone: This person is currently a member here? (Circle appropriate)   Yes   No

CHILDREN (IF APPLICABLE)

Name:	Age	Contact

About your household (What would you like the church to know about your family)

_____

_____

_____

_____

_____

_____	_____
Date	Signature

APPLICATION FOR CHURCH MEMBERSHIP FORM

PERSONAL INFORMATION

First name:	Middle:	Last:	Birthdate:

Address:	City:

State:	ZIP:	Email:

Phone:	Home phone:	Identity Number:

Tick Appropriate Box ☐ Single ☐ Married ☐ Divorced ☐ Widowed ☐ Separated ☐ Minor

Have you been baptized ? Yes ☐ No ☐ Baptism Date:	Baptism Location:

Have you been confirmed? Yes ☐ No ☐ Confirmation date:	Confirmation place:

Sex ☐ Male ☐ Female	Employer:

Work Address:	City:	State:	ZIP:

If student, Name of school:	City:	State:

Spouse/Parent's Name:	Employer:	Work Phone:

Emergency contact:	Phone:

PARENT/GUARDIAN/SPOUSE INFORMATION

Name:	Relationship:

Address:	City:	State:	Phone:

E-Mail:	Birthdate:	SSN:

Employer:	Address:

Work Phone:	This person is currently a member here? (Circle appropriate) Yes No

CHILDREN (IF APPLICABLE)

Name:	Age	Contact

About your household (What would you like the church to know about your family)

_____ _____

Date   Signature

APPLICATION FOR CHURCH MEMBERSHIP FORM

PERSONAL INFORMATION

First name:	Middle:	Last:	Birthdate:
Address:			City:
State:	ZIP:	Email:	
Phone:	Home phone:	Identity Number:	

Tick Appropriate Box ☐ Single ☐ Married ☐ Divorced ☐ Widowed ☐ Separated ☐ Minor

Have you been baptized ? Yes ☐ No ☐ Baptism Date: Baptism Location:

Have you been confirmed? Yes ☐ No ☐ Confirmation date: Confirmation place:

Sex ☐ Male ☐ Female Employer:

Work Address:	City:	State:	ZIP:
If student, Name of school:	City:	State:	
Spouse/Parent's Name:	Employer:	Work Phone:	
Emergency contact:		Phone:	

PARENT/GUARDIAN/SPOUSE INFORMATION

Name:		Relationship:	
Address:	City:	State:	Phone:
E-Mail:	Birthdate:	SSN:	
Employer:	Address:		
Work Phone:	This person is currently a member here? (Circle appropriate)	Yes	No

CHILDREN (IF APPLICABLE)

Name:	Age	Contact

About your household (What would you like the church to know about your family)

_____

_____

_____

_____

_____

Date   Signature

APPLICATION FOR CHURCH MEMBERSHIP FORM

PERSONAL INFORMATION

First name:	Middle:	Last:	Birthdate:

Address:	City:

State:	ZIP:	Email:

Phone:	Home phone:	Identity Number:

Tick Appropriate Box ☐ Single ☐ Married ☐ Divorced ☐ Widowed ☐ Separated ☐ Minor

Have you been baptized ? Yes ☐ No ☐ Baptism Date:	Baptism Location:

Have you been confirmed? Yes ☐ No ☐ Confirmation date:	Confirmation place:

Sex ☐ Male ☐ Female	Employer:

Work Address:	City:	State:	ZIP:

If student, Name of school:	City:	State:

Spouse/Parent's Name:	Employer:	Work Phone:

Emergency contact:	Phone:

PARENT/GUARDIAN/SPOUSE INFORMATION

Name:	Relationship:

Address:	City:	State:	Phone:

E-Mail:	Birthdate:	SSN:

Employer:	Address:

Work Phone:	This person is currently a member here? (Circle appropriate) Yes No

CHILDREN (IF APPLICABLE)

Name:	Age	Contact

About your household (What would you like the church to know about your family)

_____

_____

_____

_____

_____

_____

Date	Signature

APPLICATION FOR CHURCH MEMBERSHIP FORM

PERSONAL INFORMATION

First name:	Middle:	Last:	Birthdate:

Address:	City:

State:	ZIP:	Email:

Phone:	Home phone:	Identity Number:

Tick Appropriate Box ☐ Single ☐ Married ☐ Divorced ☐ Widowed ☐ Separated ☐ Minor

Have you been baptized ? Yes ☐ No ☐ Baptism Date: Baptism Location:

Have you been confirmed? Yes ☐ No ☐ Confirmation date: Confirmation place:

Sex ☐ Male ☐ Female Employer:

Work Address:	City:	State:	ZIP:

If student, Name of school:	City:	State:

Spouse/Parent's Name:	Employer:	Work Phone:

Emergency contact:	Phone:

PARENT/GUARDIAN/SPOUSE INFORMATION

Name:	Relationship:

Address:	City:	State:	Phone:

E-Mail:	Birthdate:	SSN:

Employer:	Address:

Work Phone: This person is currently a member here? (Circle appropriate)   Yes   No

CHILDREN (IF APPLICABLE)

Name:	Age	Contact

About your household (What would you like the church to know about your family)

_____

_____

_____

_____

_____

_____	_____
Date	Signature

APPLICATION FOR CHURCH MEMBERSHIP FORM

PERSONAL INFORMATION

First name:	Middle:	Last:	Birthdate:

Address: | City:

State: | ZIP: | Email:

Phone: | Home phone: | Identity Number:

Tick Appropriate Box ☐ Single ☐ Married ☐ Divorced ☐ Widowed ☐ Separated ☐ Minor

Have you been baptized ? Yes ☐ No ☐ Baptism Date: Baptism Location:

Have you been confirmed? Yes ☐ No ☐ Confirmation date: Confirmation place:

Sex ☐ Male ☐ Female | Employer:

Work Address: City: State: ZIP:

If student, Name of school: City: State:

Spouse/Parent's Name: Employer: Work Phone:

Emergency contact: Phone:

PARENT/GUARDIAN/SPOUSE INFORMATION

Name: | Relationship:

Address: City: State: | Phone:

E-Mail: | Birthdate: | SSN:

Employer: Address:

Work Phone: This person is currently a member here? (Circle appropriate) Yes No

CHILDREN (IF APPLICABLE)

Name:	Age	Contact

About your household (What would you like the church to know about your family)

_____

_____

_____

_____

_____

_____

_____   _____
Date   Signature

APPLICATION FOR CHURCH MEMBERSHIP FORM

PERSONAL INFORMATION

First name:	Middle:	Last:	Birthdate:

Address:	City:

State:	ZIP:	Email:

Phone:	Home phone:	Identity Number:

Tick Appropriate Box ☐ Single ☐ Married ☐ Divorced ☐ Widowed ☐ Separated ☐ Minor

Have you been baptized ? Yes ☐ No ☐	Baptism Date:	Baptism Location:

Have you been confirmed? Yes ☐ No ☐	Confirmation date:	Confirmation place:

Sex ☐ Male ☐ Female	Employer:

Work Address:	City:	State:	ZIP:

If student, Name of school:	City:	State:

Spouse/Parent's Name:	Employer:	Work Phone:

Emergency contact:	Phone:

PARENT/GUARDIAN/SPOUSE INFORMATION

Name:	Relationship:

Address:	City:	State:	Phone:

E-Mail:	Birthdate:	SSN:

Employer:	Address:

Work Phone:	This person is currently a member here? (Circle appropriate)	Yes No

CHILDREN (IF APPLICABLE)

Name:	Age	Contact

About your household (What would you like the church to know about your family)

_____

_____

_____

_____

_____

_____   _____
Date   Signature

APPLICATION FOR CHURCH MEMBERSHIP FORM

PERSONAL INFORMATION

First name:	Middle:	Last:	Birthdate:

Address: | City:

State: | ZIP: | Email:

Phone: | Home phone: | Identity Number:

Tick Appropriate Box ☐ Single ☐ Married ☐ Divorced ☐ Widowed ☐ Separated ☐ Minor

Have you been baptized ? Yes ☐ No ☐ Baptism Date: | Baptism Location:

Have you been confirmed? Yes ☐ No ☐ Confirmation date: | Confirmation place:

Sex ☐ Male ☐ Female | Employer:

Work Address: | City: | State: | ZIP:

If student, Name of school: | City: | State:

Spouse/Parent's Name: | Employer: | Work Phone:

Emergency contact: | Phone:

PARENT/GUARDIAN/SPOUSE INFORMATION

Name: | Relationship:

Address: | City: | State: | Phone:

E-Mail: | Birthdate: | SSN:

Employer: | Address:

Work Phone: | This person is currently a member here? (Circle appropriate) Yes No

CHILDREN (IF APPLICABLE)

Name:	Age	Contact

About your household (What would you like the church to know about your family)

_____

_____

_____

_____

_____

_____

Date | Signature

APPLICATION FOR CHURCH MEMBERSHIP FORM

PERSONAL INFORMATION

First name:	Middle:	Last:	Birthdate:

Address: | City:

State: | ZIP: | Email:

Phone: | Home phone: | Identity Number:

Tick Appropriate Box ☐ Single ☐ Married ☐ Divorced ☐ Widowed ☐ Separated ☐ Minor

Have you been baptized ? Yes ☐ No ☐ Baptism Date: | Baptism Location:

Have you been confirmed? Yes ☐ No ☐ Confirmation date: | Confirmation place:

Sex ☐ Male ☐ Female | Employer:

Work Address: | City: | State: | ZIP:

If student, Name of school: | City: | State:

Spouse/Parent's Name: | Employer: | Work Phone:

Emergency contact: | Phone:

PARENT/GUARDIAN/SPOUSE INFORMATION

Name: | Relationship:

Address: | City: | State: | Phone:

E-Mail: | Birthdate: | SSN:

Employer: | Address:

Work Phone: | This person is currently a member here? (Circle appropriate)   Yes   No

CHILDREN (IF APPLICABLE)

Name:	Age	Contact

About your household (What would you like the church to know about your family)

_____

_____

_____

_____

_____   _____
Date   Signature

APPLICATION FOR CHURCH MEMBERSHIP FORM

PERSONAL INFORMATION

First name:	Middle:	Last:	Birthdate:

First name: Middle: Last: Birthdate:

Address: City:

State: ZIP: Email:

Phone: Home phone: Identity Number:

Tick Appropriate Box ☐ Single ☐ Married ☐ Divorced ☐ Widowed ☐ Separated ☐ Minor

Have you been baptized ?   Yes ☐   No ☐   Baptism Date: Baptism Location:

Have you been confirmed?   Yes ☐   No ☐   Confirmation date: Confirmation place:

Sex ☐ Male ☐ Female   Employer:

Work Address: City: State: ZIP:

If student, Name of school: City: State:

Spouse/Parent's Name: Employer: Work Phone:

Emergency contact: Phone:

PARENT/GUARDIAN/SPOUSE INFORMATION

Name: Relationship:

Address: City: State: Phone:

E-Mail: Birthdate: SSN:

Employer: Address:

Work Phone: This person is currently a member here? (Circle appropriate)   Yes   No

CHILDREN (IF APPLICABLE)

Name:	Age	Contact

About your household (What would you like the church to know about your family)

_____

_____

_____

_____

_____

Date   Signature

APPLICATION FOR CHURCH MEMBERSHIP FORM

PERSONAL INFORMATION

First name:	Middle:	Last:	Birthdate:

Address:	City:

State:	ZIP:	Email:

Phone:	Home phone:	Identity Number:

Tick Appropriate Box ☐ Single ☐ Married ☐ Divorced ☐ Widowed ☐ Separated ☐ Minor

Have you been baptized ? Yes ☐ No ☐	Baptism Date:	Baptism Location:

Have you been confirmed? Yes ☐ No ☐	Confirmation date:	Confirmation place:

Sex ☐ Male ☐ Female	Employer:

Work Address:	City:	State:	ZIP:

If student, Name of school:	City:	State:

Spouse/Parent's Name:	Employer:	Work Phone:

Emergency contact:	Phone:

PARENT/GUARDIAN/SPOUSE INFORMATION

Name:	Relationship:

Address:	City:	State:	Phone:

E-Mail:	Birthdate:	SSN:

Employer:	Address:

Work Phone: This person is currently a member here? (Circle appropriate)   Yes   No

CHILDREN (IF APPLICABLE)

Name:	Age	Contact

About your household (What would you like the church to know about your family)

_____

_____

_____

_____

_____

_____	_____
Date	Signature

APPLICATION FOR CHURCH MEMBERSHIP FORM

PERSONAL INFORMATION

First name:	Middle:	Last:	Birthdate:

Address:	City:

State:	ZIP:	Email:

Phone:	Home phone:	Identity Number:

Tick Appropriate Box ☐ Single ☐ Married ☐ Divorced ☐ Widowed ☐ Separated ☐ Minor

Have you been baptized ? Yes ☐ No ☐ Baptism Date: Baptism Location:

Have you been confirmed? Yes ☐ No ☐ Confirmation date: Confirmation place:

Sex ☐ Male ☐ Female Employer:

Work Address:	City:	State:	ZIP:

If student, Name of school:	City:	State:

Spouse/Parent's Name:	Employer:	Work Phone:

Emergency contact:	Phone:

PARENT/GUARDIAN/SPOUSE INFORMATION

Name:	Relationship:

Address:	City:	State:	Phone:

E-Mail:	Birthdate:	SSN:

Employer:	Address:

Work Phone: This person is currently a member here? (Circle appropriate) Yes No

CHILDREN (IF APPLICABLE)

Name:	Age	Contact

About your household (What would you like the church to know about your family)

_____

_____

_____

_____

_____

_____   _____
Date   Signature

APPLICATION FOR CHURCH MEMBERSHIP FORM

PERSONAL INFORMATION

First name:	Middle:	Last:	Birthdate:

Address:	City:

State:	ZIP:	Email:

Phone:	Home phone:	Identity Number:

Tick Appropriate Box ☐ Single ☐ Married ☐ Divorced ☐ Widowed ☐ Separated ☐ Minor

Have you been baptized ? Yes ☐ No ☐	Baptism Date:	Baptism Location:

Have you been confirmed? Yes ☐ No ☐	Confirmation date:	Confirmation place:

Sex ☐ Male ☐ Female	Employer:

Work Address:	City:	State:	ZIP:

If student, Name of school:	City:	State:

Spouse/Parent's Name:	Employer:	Work Phone:

Emergency contact:	Phone:

PARENT/GUARDIAN/SPOUSE INFORMATION

Name:	Relationship:

Address:	City:	State:	Phone:

E-Mail:	Birthdate:	SSN:

Employer:	Address:

Work Phone:	This person is currently a member here? (Circle appropriate) Yes No

CHILDREN (IF APPLICABLE)

Name:	Age	Contact

About your household (What would you like the church to know about your family)

_____

_____

_____

_____

_____

_____	_____
Date	Signature

APPLICATION FOR CHURCH MEMBERSHIP FORM

PERSONAL INFORMATION

First name:	Middle:	Last:	Birthdate:
Address:			City:
State:	ZIP:	Email:	
Phone:	Home phone:	Identity Number:	

Tick Appropriate Box ☐ Single ☐ Married ☐ Divorced ☐ Widowed ☐ Separated ☐ Minor

Have you been baptized ? Yes ☐ No ☐ Baptism Date: Baptism Location:

Have you been confirmed? Yes ☐ No ☐ Confirmation date: Confirmation place:

Sex ☐ Male ☐ Female Employer:

Work Address:	City:	State:	ZIP:
If student, Name of school:	City:	State:	
Spouse/Parent's Name:	Employer:	Work Phone:	
Emergency contact:	Phone:		

PARENT/GUARDIAN/SPOUSE INFORMATION

Name:	Relationship:	
Address:	City: State:	Phone:
E-Mail:	Birthdate:	SSN:
Employer:	Address:	
Work Phone:	This person is currently a member here? (Circle appropriate)	Yes No

CHILDREN (IF APPLICABLE)

Name:	Age	Contact

About your household (What would you like the church to know about your family)

_____

_____

_____

_____

_____

Date	Signature

APPLICATION FOR CHURCH MEMBERSHIP FORM

PERSONAL INFORMATION

First name:	Middle:	Last:	Birthdate:

Address: | City:

State: | ZIP: | Email:

Phone: | Home phone: | Identity Number:

Tick Appropriate Box ☐ Single ☐ Married ☐ Divorced ☐ Widowed ☐ Separated ☐ Minor

Have you been baptized ? Yes ☐   No ☐   Baptism Date: | Baptism Location:

Have you been confirmed?   Yes ☐   No ☐   Confirmation date: | Confirmation place:

Sex ☐ Male ☐ Female | Employer:

Work Address: | City: | State: | ZIP:

If student, Name of school: | City: | State:

Spouse/Parent's Name: | Employer: | Work Phone:

Emergency contact: | Phone:

PARENT/GUARDIAN/SPOUSE INFORMATION

Name: | Relationship:

Address: | City: | State: | Phone:

E-Mail: | Birthdate: | SSN:

Employer: | Address:

Work Phone: | This person is currently a member here? (Circle appropriate)   Yes   No

CHILDREN (IF APPLICABLE)

Name:	Age	Contact

About your household (What would you like the church to know about your family)

_____

_____

_____

_____

_____

Date

Signature

APPLICATION FOR CHURCH MEMBERSHIP FORM

PERSONAL INFORMATION

First name: | Middle: | Last: | Birthdate:

Address: | City:

State: | ZIP: | Email:

Phone: | Home phone: | Identity Number:

Tick Appropriate Box ☐ Single ☐ Married ☐ Divorced ☐ Widowed ☐ Separated ☐ Minor

Have you been baptized ? Yes ☐ No ☐ Baptism Date: | Baptism Location:

Have you been confirmed? Yes ☐ No ☐ Confirmation date: | Confirmation place:

Sex ☐ Male ☐ Female | Employer:

Work Address: | City: | State: | ZIP:

If student, Name of school: | City: | State:

Spouse/Parent's Name: | Employer: | Work Phone:

Emergency contact: | Phone:

PARENT/GUARDIAN/SPOUSE INFORMATION

Name: | Relationship:

Address: | City: | State: | Phone:

E-Mail: | Birthdate: | SSN:

Employer: | Address:

Work Phone: | This person is currently a member here? (Circle appropriate) | Yes | No

CHILDREN (IF APPLICABLE)

Name:	Age	Contact

About your household (What would you like the church to know about your family)

_____

_____

_____

_____

_____

_____   _____
Date   Signature

APPLICATION FOR CHURCH MEMBERSHIP FORM

PERSONAL INFORMATION

First name:	Middle:	Last:	Birthdate:

Address:	City:

State:	ZIP:	Email:

Phone:	Home phone:	Identity Number:

Tick Appropriate Box ☐ Single ☐ Married ☐ Divorced ☐ Widowed ☐ Separated ☐ Minor

Have you been baptized ? Yes ☐ No ☐ Baptism Date: Baptism Location:

Have you been confirmed? Yes ☐ No ☐ Confirmation date: Confirmation place:

Sex ☐ Male ☐ Female | Employer:

Work Address:	City:	State:	ZIP:

If student, Name of school:	City:	State:

Spouse/Parent's Name:	Employer:	Work Phone:

Emergency contact:	Phone:

PARENT/GUARDIAN/SPOUSE INFORMATION

Name:	Relationship:

Address:	City:	State:	Phone:

E-Mail:	Birthdate:	SSN:

Employer:	Address:

Work Phone: | This person is currently a member here? (Circle appropriate)   Yes   No

CHILDREN (IF APPLICABLE)

Name:	Age	Contact

About your household (What would you like the church to know about your family)

_____

_____

_____

_____

_____

_____   _____
Date   Signature

APPLICATION FOR CHURCH MEMBERSHIP FORM

PERSONAL INFORMATION

First name:	Middle:	Last:	Birthdate:
Address:			City:
State:	ZIP:	Email:	
Phone:	Home phone:		Identity Number:

Tick Appropriate Box ☐ Single ☐ Married ☐ Divorced ☐ Widowed ☐ Separated ☐ Minor

Have you been baptized ? Yes ☐ No ☐ Baptism Date: Baptism Location:

Have you been confirmed? Yes ☐ No ☐ Confirmation date: Confirmation place:

Sex ☐ Male ☐ Female Employer:

Work Address:	City:	State:	ZIP:
If student, Name of school:	City:	State:	
Spouse/Parent's Name:	Employer:	Work Phone:	
Emergency contact:		Phone:	

PARENT/GUARDIAN/SPOUSE INFORMATION

Name:			Relationship:
Address:	City:	State:	Phone:
E-Mail:		Birthdate:	SSN:
Employer:		Address:	
Work Phone:	This person is currently a member here? (Circle appropriate)	Yes	No

CHILDREN (IF APPLICABLE)

Name:	Age	Contact

About your household (What would you like the church to know about your family)

_____

_____

_____

_____

_____

_____   _____
Date   Signature

APPLICATION FOR CHURCH MEMBERSHIP FORM

PERSONAL INFORMATION

First name:	Middle:	Last:	Birthdate:

Address: | City:

State: | ZIP: | Email:

Phone: | Home phone: | Identity Number:

Tick Appropriate Box ☐ Single ☐ Married ☐ Divorced ☐ Widowed ☐ Separated ☐ Minor

Have you been baptized ? Yes ☐ No ☐ | Baptism Date: | Baptism Location:

Have you been confirmed? Yes ☐ No ☐ | Confirmation date: | Confirmation place:

Sex ☐ Male ☐ Female | Employer:

Work Address: | City: | State: | ZIP:

If student, Name of school: | City: | State:

Spouse/Parent's Name: | Employer: | Work Phone:

Emergency contact: | Phone:

PARENT/GUARDIAN/SPOUSE INFORMATION

Name: | Relationship:

Address: | City: | State: | Phone:

E-Mail: | Birthdate: | SSN:

Employer: | Address:

Work Phone: | This person is currently a member here? (Circle appropriate) | Yes | No

CHILDREN (IF APPLICABLE)

Name:	Age	Contact

About your household (What would you like the church to know about your family)

_____

_____

_____

_____

_____

Date | Signature

APPLICATION FOR CHURCH MEMBERSHIP FORM

PERSONAL INFORMATION

First name:	Middle:	Last:	Birthdate:

Address:	City:

State:	ZIP:	Email:

Phone:	Home phone:	Identity Number:

Tick Appropriate Box ☐ Single ☐ Married ☐ Divorced ☐ Widowed ☐ Separated ☐ Minor

Have you been baptized ? Yes ☐ No ☐ Baptism Date: Baptism Location:

Have you been confirmed? Yes ☐ No ☐ Confirmation date: Confirmation place:

Sex ☐ Male ☐ Female	Employer:

Work Address:	City:	State:	ZIP:

If student, Name of school:	City:	State:

Spouse/Parent's Name:	Employer:	Work Phone:

Emergency contact:	Phone:

PARENT/GUARDIAN/SPOUSE INFORMATION

Name:	Relationship:

Address:	City:	State:	Phone:

E-Mail:	Birthdate:	SSN:

Employer:	Address:

Work Phone:	This person is currently a member here? (Circle appropriate)	Yes No

CHILDREN (IF APPLICABLE)

Name:	Age	Contact

About your household (What would you like the church to know about your family)

_____

_____

_____

_____

_____

_____	_____
Date	Signature

APPLICATION FOR CHURCH MEMBERSHIP FORM

PERSONAL INFORMATION

First name:	Middle:	Last:	Birthdate:

Address:	City:

State:	ZIP:	Email:

Phone:	Home phone:	Identity Number:

Tick Appropriate Box ☐ Single ☐ Married ☐ Divorced ☐ Widowed ☐ Separated ☐ Minor

Have you been baptized ? Yes ☐ No ☐ Baptism Date: Baptism Location:

Have you been confirmed? Yes ☐ No ☐ Confirmation date: Confirmation place:

Sex ☐ Male ☐ Female Employer:

Work Address:	City:	State:	ZIP:

If student, Name of school:	City:	State:

Spouse/Parent's Name:	Employer:	Work Phone:

Emergency contact:	Phone:

PARENT/GUARDIAN/SPOUSE INFORMATION

Name:	Relationship:

Address:	City:	State:	Phone:

E-Mail:	Birthdate:	SSN:

Employer:	Address:

Work Phone: This person is currently a member here? (Circle appropriate)   Yes   No

CHILDREN (IF APPLICABLE)

Name:	Age	Contact

About your household (What would you like the church to know about your family)

_____
_____
_____
_____
_____

_____   _____
Date   Signature

APPLICATION FOR CHURCH MEMBERSHIP FORM

PERSONAL INFORMATION

First name:	Middle:	Last:	Birthdate:

Address:	City:

State:	ZIP:	Email:

Phone:	Home phone:	Identity Number:

Tick Appropriate Box ☐ Single ☐ Married ☐ Divorced ☐ Widowed ☐ Separated ☐ Minor

Have you been baptized ? Yes ☐ No ☐ Baptism Date: Baptism Location:

Have you been confirmed? Yes ☐ No ☐ Confirmation date: Confirmation place:

Sex ☐ Male ☐ Female | Employer:

Work Address:	City:	State:	ZIP:

If student, Name of school:	City:	State:

Spouse/Parent's Name:	Employer:	Work Phone:

Emergency contact:	Phone:

PARENT/GUARDIAN/SPOUSE INFORMATION

Name:	Relationship:

Address:	City:	State:	Phone:

E-Mail:	Birthdate:	SSN:

Employer:	Address:

Work Phone: | This person is currently a member here? (Circle appropriate)   Yes   No

CHILDREN (IF APPLICABLE)

Name:	Age	Contact

About your household (What would you like the church to know about your family)

_____

_____

_____

_____

_____

_____

_____   _____
Date   Signature

APPLICATION FOR CHURCH MEMBERSHIP FORM

PERSONAL INFORMATION

First name: Middle: Last: Birthdate:

Address: City:

State: ZIP: Email:

Phone: Home phone: Identity Number:

Tick Appropriate Box ☐ Single ☐ Married ☐ Divorced ☐ Widowed ☐ Separated ☐ Minor

Have you been baptized ? Yes ☐   No ☐   Baptism Date: Baptism Location:

Have you been confirmed? Yes ☐   No ☐   Confirmation date: Confirmation place:

Sex ☐ Male ☐ Female   Employer:

Work Address: City: State: ZIP:

If student, Name of school: City: State:

Spouse/Parent's Name: Employer: Work Phone:

Emergency contact: Phone:

PARENT/GUARDIAN/SPOUSE INFORMATION

Name: Relationship:

Address: City: State: Phone:

E-Mail: Birthdate: SSN:

Employer: Address:

Work Phone: This person is currently a member here? (Circle appropriate)   Yes   No

CHILDREN (IF APPLICABLE)

Name:	Age	Contact

About your household (What would you like the church to know about your family)

_____

_____

_____

_____

_____

Date   Signature

APPLICATION FOR CHURCH MEMBERSHIP FORM

PERSONAL INFORMATION

First name:	Middle:	Last:	Birthdate:

Address:	City:

State:	ZIP:	Email:

Phone:	Home phone:	Identity Number:

Tick Appropriate Box ☐ Single ☐ Married ☐ Divorced ☐ Widowed ☐ Separated ☐ Minor

Have you been baptized ? Yes ☐ No ☐   Baptism Date: _____   Baptism Location: _____

Have you been confirmed? Yes ☐ No ☐   Confirmation date: _____   Confirmation place: _____

Sex ☐ Male ☐ Female   Employer: _____

Work Address:	City:	State:	ZIP:

If student, Name of school:	City:	State:

Spouse/Parent's Name:	Employer:	Work Phone:

Emergency contact:	Phone:

PARENT/GUARDIAN/SPOUSE INFORMATION

Name:	Relationship:

Address:	City:	State:	Phone:

E-Mail:	Birthdate:	SSN:

Employer:	Address:

Work Phone:	This person is currently a member here? (Circle appropriate) Yes No

CHILDREN (IF APPLICABLE)

Name:	Age	Contact

About your household (What would you like the church to know about your family)

_____

_____

_____

_____

_____

Date	Signature

APPLICATION FOR CHURCH MEMBERSHIP FORM

PERSONAL INFORMATION

First name:	Middle:	Last:	Birthdate:

Address: | City:

State: | ZIP: | Email:

Phone: | Home phone: | Identity Number:

Tick Appropriate Box ☐ Single ☐ Married ☐ Divorced ☐ Widowed ☐ Separated ☐ Minor

Have you been baptized ?   Yes ☐   No ☐   Baptism Date: | Baptism Location:

Have you been confirmed?   Yes ☐   No ☐   Confirmation date: | Confirmation place:

Sex ☐ Male ☐ Female | Employer:

Work Address: | City: | State: | ZIP:

If student, Name of school: | City: | State:

Spouse/Parent's Name: | Employer: | Work Phone:

Emergency contact: | Phone:

PARENT/GUARDIAN/SPOUSE INFORMATION

Name: | Relationship:

Address: | City: | State: | Phone:

E-Mail: | Birthdate: | SSN:

Employer: | Address:

Work Phone: | This person is currently a member here? (Circle appropriate)   Yes   No

CHILDREN (IF APPLICABLE)

Name:	Age	Contact

About your household (What would you like the church to know about your family)

_____

_____

_____

_____

_____

Date | Signature

APPLICATION FOR CHURCH MEMBERSHIP FORM

PERSONAL INFORMATION

First name:	Middle:	Last:	Birthdate:

Address:	City:

State:	ZIP:	Email:

Phone:	Home phone:	Identity Number:

Tick Appropriate Box ☐ Single ☐ Married ☐ Divorced ☐ Widowed ☐ Separated ☐ Minor

Have you been baptized ? Yes ☐ No ☐ Baptism Date: Baptism Location:

Have you been confirmed? Yes ☐ No ☐ Confirmation date: Confirmation place:

Sex ☐ Male ☐ Female Employer:

Work Address:	City:	State:	ZIP:

If student, Name of school:	City:	State:

Spouse/Parent's Name:	Employer:	Work Phone:

Emergency contact:	Phone:

PARENT/GUARDIAN/SPOUSE INFORMATION

Name:	Relationship:

Address:	City:	State:	Phone:

E-Mail:	Birthdate:	SSN:

Employer:	Address:

Work Phone:	This person is currently a member here? (Circle appropriate)	Yes	No

CHILDREN (IF APPLICABLE)

Name:	Age	Contact

About your household (What would you like the church to know about your family)

_____

_____

_____

_____

_____

_____   _____
Date   Signature

APPLICATION FOR CHURCH MEMBERSHIP FORM

PERSONAL INFORMATION

First name:	Middle:	Last:	Birthdate:

Address:	City:

State:	ZIP:	Email:

Phone:	Home phone:	Identity Number:

Tick Appropriate Box ☐ Single ☐ Married ☐ Divorced ☐ Widowed ☐ Separated ☐ Minor

Have you been baptized ? Yes ☐ No ☐ Baptism Date:	Baptism Location:

Have you been confirmed? Yes ☐ No ☐ Confirmation date:	Confirmation place:

Sex ☐ Male ☐ Female	Employer:

Work Address:	City:	State:	ZIP:

If student, Name of school:	City:	State:

Spouse/Parent's Name:	Employer:	Work Phone:

Emergency contact:	Phone:

PARENT/GUARDIAN/SPOUSE INFORMATION

Name:	Relationship:

Address:	City:	State:	Phone:

E-Mail:	Birthdate:	SSN:

Employer:	Address:

Work Phone: This person is currently a member here? (Circle appropriate)   Yes   No

CHILDREN (IF APPLICABLE)

Name:	Age	Contact

About your household (What would you like the church to know about your family)

_____

_____

_____

_____

_____

_____

_____   _____
Date   Signature

APPLICATION FOR CHURCH MEMBERSHIP FORM

PERSONAL INFORMATION

First name:	Middle:	Last:	Birthdate:

Address:	City:

State:	ZIP:	Email:

Phone:	Home phone:	Identity Number:

Tick Appropriate Box ☐ Single ☐ Married ☐ Divorced ☐ Widowed ☐ Separated ☐ Minor

Have you been baptized ? Yes ☐ No ☐ Baptism Date: Baptism Location:

Have you been confirmed? Yes ☐ No ☐ Confirmation date: Confirmation place:

Sex ☐ Male ☐ Female Employer:

Work Address:	City:	State:	ZIP:

If student, Name of school:	City:	State:

Spouse/Parent's Name:	Employer:	Work Phone:

Emergency contact:	Phone:

PARENT/GUARDIAN/SPOUSE INFORMATION

Name:	Relationship:

Address:	City:	State:	Phone:

E-Mail:	Birthdate:	SSN:

Employer:	Address:

Work Phone: This person is currently a member here? (Circle appropriate)   Yes   No

CHILDREN (IF APPLICABLE)

Name:	Age	Contact

About your household (What would you like the church to know about your family)

_____

_____

_____

_____

_____

_____   _____
Date   Signature

APPLICATION FOR CHURCH MEMBERSHIP FORM

PERSONAL INFORMATION

First name:	Middle:	Last:	Birthdate:

Address: | City:

State: | ZIP: | Email:

Phone: | Home phone: | Identity Number:

Tick Appropriate Box ☐ Single ☐ Married ☐ Divorced ☐ Widowed ☐ Separated ☐ Minor

Have you been baptized ? Yes ☐ No ☐ Baptism Date: | Baptism Location:

Have you been confirmed? Yes ☐ No ☐ Confirmation date: | Confirmation place:

Sex ☐ Male ☐ Female | Employer:

Work Address: | City: | State: | ZIP:

If student, Name of school: | City: | State:

Spouse/Parent's Name: | Employer: | Work Phone:

Emergency contact: | Phone:

PARENT/GUARDIAN/SPOUSE INFORMATION

Name: | Relationship:

Address: | City: | State: | Phone:

E-Mail: | Birthdate: | SSN:

Employer: | Address:

Work Phone: | This person is currently a member here? (Circle appropriate)   Yes   No

CHILDREN (IF APPLICABLE)

Name:	Age	Contact

About your household (What would you like the church to know about your family)

_____

_____

_____

_____

_____

_____   _____
Date   Signature

APPLICATION FOR CHURCH MEMBERSHIP FORM

PERSONAL INFORMATION

First name:	Middle:	Last:	Birthdate:
Address:			City:
State:	ZIP:	Email:	
Phone:	Home phone:		Identity Number:

Tick Appropriate Box ☐ Single ☐ Married ☐ Divorced ☐ Widowed ☐ Separated ☐ Minor

Have you been baptized ? Yes ☐ No ☐ Baptism Date: Baptism Location:

Have you been confirmed? Yes ☐ No ☐ Confirmation date: Confirmation place:

Sex ☐ Male ☐ Female Employer:

Work Address:	City:	State:	ZIP:
If student, Name of school:		City:	State:
Spouse/Parent's Name:	Employer:	Work Phone:	
Emergency contact:		Phone:	

PARENT/GUARDIAN/SPOUSE INFORMATION

Name:			Relationship:
Address:	City:	State:	Phone:
E-Mail:	Birthdate:		SSN:
Employer:		Address:	
Work Phone:	This person is currently a member here? (Circle appropriate) Yes No		

CHILDREN (IF APPLICABLE)

Name:	Age	Contact

About your household (What would you like the church to know about your family)

_____

_____

_____

_____

_____

_____   _____
Date   Signature

APPLICATION FOR CHURCH MEMBERSHIP FORM

PERSONAL INFORMATION

First name: | Middle: | Last: | Birthdate:

Address: | City:

State: | ZIP: | Email:

Phone: | Home phone: | Identity Number:

Tick Appropriate Box ☐ Single ☐ Married ☐ Divorced ☐ Widowed ☐ Separated ☐ Minor

Have you been baptized ? Yes ☐   No ☐   Baptism Date: | Baptism Location:

Have you been confirmed? Yes ☐   No ☐   Confirmation date: | Confirmation place:

Sex ☐ Male ☐ Female | Employer:

Work Address: | City: | State: | ZIP:

If student, Name of school: | City: | State:

Spouse/Parent's Name: | Employer: | Work Phone:

Emergency contact: | Phone:

PARENT/GUARDIAN/SPOUSE INFORMATION

Name: | Relationship:

Address: | City: | State: | Phone:

E-Mail: | Birthdate: | SSN:

Employer: | Address:

Work Phone: | This person is currently a member here? (Circle appropriate)   Yes   No

CHILDREN (IF APPLICABLE)

Name:	Age	Contact

About your household (What would you like the church to know about your family)

_____

_____

_____

_____

_____

Date | Signature

APPLICATION FOR CHURCH MEMBERSHIP FORM

PERSONAL INFORMATION

First name:	Middle:	Last:	Birthdate:

Address:	City:

State:	ZIP:	Email:

Phone:	Home phone:	Identity Number:

Tick Appropriate Box ☐ Single ☐ Married ☐ Divorced ☐ Widowed ☐ Separated ☐ Minor

Have you been baptized ? Yes ☐ No ☐ Baptism Date: Baptism Location:

Have you been confirmed? Yes ☐ No ☐ Confirmation date: Confirmation place:

Sex ☐ Male ☐ Female Employer:

Work Address:	City:	State:	ZIP:

If student, Name of school:	City:	State:

Spouse/Parent's Name:	Employer:	Work Phone:

Emergency contact:	Phone:

PARENT/GUARDIAN/SPOUSE INFORMATION

Name:	Relationship:

Address:	City:	State:	Phone:

E-Mail:	Birthdate:	SSN:

Employer:	Address:

Work Phone: This person is currently a member here? (Circle appropriate) Yes No

CHILDREN (IF APPLICABLE)

Name:	Age	Contact

About your household (What would you like the church to know about your family)

_____

_____

_____

_____

_____

_____

_____   _____
Date   Signature

APPLICATION FOR CHURCH MEMBERSHIP FORM

PERSONAL INFORMATION

First name:	Middle:	Last:	Birthdate:

Address: | City:

State: | ZIP: | Email:

Phone: | Home phone: | Identity Number:

Tick Appropriate Box ☐ Single ☐ Married ☐ Divorced ☐ Widowed ☐ Separated ☐ Minor

Have you been baptized ? Yes ☐ No ☐ Baptism Date: | Baptism Location:

Have you been confirmed? Yes ☐ No ☐ Confirmation date: | Confirmation place:

Sex ☐ Male ☐ Female | Employer:

Work Address: | City: | State: | ZIP:

If student, Name of school: | City: | State:

Spouse/Parent's Name: | Employer: | Work Phone:

Emergency contact: | Phone:

PARENT/GUARDIAN/SPOUSE INFORMATION

Name: | Relationship:

Address: | City: | State: | Phone:

E-Mail: | Birthdate: | SSN:

Employer: | Address:

Work Phone: | This person is currently a member here? (Circle appropriate) Yes No

CHILDREN (IF APPLICABLE)

Name:	Age	Contact

About your household (What would you like the church to know about your family)

_____

_____

_____

_____

_____   _____
Date   Signature

APPLICATION FOR CHURCH MEMBERSHIP FORM

PERSONAL INFORMATION

First name:	Middle:	Last:	Birthdate:

Address:	City:

State:	ZIP:	Email:

Phone:	Home phone:	Identity Number:

Tick Appropriate Box ☐ Single ☐ Married ☐ Divorced ☐ Widowed ☐ Separated ☐ Minor

Have you been baptized ? Yes ☐ No ☐	Baptism Date:	Baptism Location:

Have you been confirmed? Yes ☐ No ☐	Confirmation date:	Confirmation place:

Sex ☐ Male ☐ Female	Employer:

Work Address:	City:	State:	ZIP:

If student, Name of school:	City:	State:

Spouse/Parent's Name:	Employer:	Work Phone:

Emergency contact:	Phone:

PARENT/GUARDIAN/SPOUSE INFORMATION

Name:	Relationship:

Address:	City:	State:	Phone:

E-Mail:	Birthdate:	SSN:

Employer:	Address:

Work Phone:	This person is currently a member here? (Circle appropriate) Yes No

CHILDREN (IF APPLICABLE)

Name:	Age	Contact

About your household (What would you like the church to know about your family)

_____

_____

_____

_____

_____

_____   _____
Date   Signature

APPLICATION FOR CHURCH MEMBERSHIP FORM

PERSONAL INFORMATION

First name:	Middle:	Last:	Birthdate:

Address:	City:

State:	ZIP:	Email:

Phone:	Home phone:	Identity Number:

Tick Appropriate Box ☐ Single ☐ Married ☐ Divorced ☐ Widowed ☐ Separated ☐ Minor

Have you been baptized ? Yes ☐ No ☐ Baptism Date: Baptism Location:

Have you been confirmed? Yes ☐ No ☐ Confirmation date: Confirmation place:

Sex ☐ Male ☐ Female Employer:

Work Address:	City:	State:	ZIP:

If student, Name of school:	City:	State:

Spouse/Parent's Name:	Employer:	Work Phone:

Emergency contact:	Phone:

PARENT/GUARDIAN/SPOUSE INFORMATION

Name:	Relationship:

Address:	City:	State:	Phone:

E-Mail:	Birthdate:	SSN:

Employer:	Address:

Work Phone: This person is currently a member here? (Circle appropriate) Yes No

CHILDREN (IF APPLICABLE)

Name:	Age	Contact

About your household (What would you like the church to know about your family)

_____

_____

_____

_____

_____

_____   _____
Date   Signature

APPLICATION FOR CHURCH MEMBERSHIP FORM

PERSONAL INFORMATION

First name:	Middle:	Last:	Birthdate:

Address: | City:

State: | ZIP: | Email:

Phone: | Home phone: | Identity Number:

Tick Appropriate Box ☐ Single ☐ Married ☐ Divorced ☐ Widowed ☐ Separated ☐ Minor

Have you been baptized ? Yes ☐ No ☐ Baptism Date: | Baptism Location:

Have you been confirmed? Yes ☐ No ☐ Confirmation date: | Confirmation place:

Sex ☐ Male ☐ Female | Employer:

Work Address: | City: | State: | ZIP:

If student, Name of school: | City: | State:

Spouse/Parent's Name: | Employer: | Work Phone:

Emergency contact: | Phone:

PARENT/GUARDIAN/SPOUSE INFORMATION

Name: | Relationship:

Address: | City: | State: | Phone:

E-Mail: | Birthdate: | SSN:

Employer: | Address:

Work Phone: | This person is currently a member here? (Circle appropriate)   Yes   No

CHILDREN (IF APPLICABLE)

Name:	Age	Contact

About your household (What would you like the church to know about your family)

_____

_____

_____

_____

_____   _____
Date   Signature

APPLICATION FOR CHURCH MEMBERSHIP FORM

PERSONAL INFORMATION

First name:	Middle:	Last:	Birthdate:

Address: | City:

State: | ZIP: | Email:

Phone: | Home phone: | Identity Number:

Tick Appropriate Box ☐ Single ☐ Married ☐ Divorced ☐ Widowed ☐ Separated ☐ Minor

Have you been baptized ? Yes ☐ No ☐ Baptism Date: | Baptism Location:

Have you been confirmed? Yes ☐ No ☐ Confirmation date: | Confirmation place:

Sex ☐ Male ☐ Female | Employer:

Work Address: | City: | State: | ZIP:

If student, Name of school: | City: | State:

Spouse/Parent's Name: | Employer: | Work Phone:

Emergency contact: | Phone:

PARENT/GUARDIAN/SPOUSE INFORMATION

Name: | Relationship:

Address: | City: | State: | Phone:

E-Mail: | Birthdate: | SSN:

Employer: | Address:

Work Phone: | This person is currently a member here? (Circle appropriate) | Yes | No

CHILDREN (IF APPLICABLE)

Name:	Age	Contact

About your household (What would you like the church to know about your family)

_____

_____

_____

_____

_____

_____

Date

_____

Signature

APPLICATION FOR CHURCH MEMBERSHIP FORM

PERSONAL INFORMATION

First name:	Middle:	Last:	Birthdate:

Address:	City:

State:	ZIP:	Email:

Phone:	Home phone:	Identity Number:

Tick Appropriate Box ☐ Single ☐ Married ☐ Divorced ☐ Widowed ☐ Separated ☐ Minor

Have you been baptized ? Yes ☐ No ☐ Baptism Date: Baptism Location:

Have you been confirmed? Yes ☐ No ☐ Confirmation date: Confirmation place:

Sex ☐ Male ☐ Female Employer:

Work Address:	City:	State:	ZIP:

If student, Name of school: City: State:

Spouse/Parent's Name: Employer: Work Phone:

Emergency contact: Phone:

PARENT/GUARDIAN/SPOUSE INFORMATION

Name:	Relationship:

Address:	City:	State:	Phone:

E-Mail:	Birthdate:	SSN:

Employer:	Address:

Work Phone: This person is currently a member here? (Circle appropriate) Yes No

CHILDREN (IF APPLICABLE)

Name:	Age	Contact

About your household (What would you like the church to know about your family)

_____

_____

_____

_____

_____

Date	Signature

APPLICATION FOR CHURCH MEMBERSHIP FORM

PERSONAL INFORMATION

First name:	Middle:	Last:	Birthdate:
Address:		City:	
State:	ZIP:	Email:	
Phone:	Home phone:	Identity Number:	

Tick Appropriate Box ☐ Single ☐ Married ☐ Divorced ☐ Widowed ☐ Separated ☐ Minor

Have you been baptized ? Yes ☐ No ☐ Baptism Date:	Baptism Location:	
Have you been confirmed? Yes ☐ No ☐ Confirmation date:	Confirmation place:	
Sex ☐ Male ☐ Female	Employer:	
Work Address:	City: State: ZIP:	
If student, Name of school:	City: State:	
Spouse/Parent's Name:	Employer:	Work Phone:
Emergency contact:	Phone:	

PARENT/GUARDIAN/SPOUSE INFORMATION

Name:	Relationship:
Address: City: State:	Phone:
E-Mail: Birthdate:	SSN:
Employer: Address:	
Work Phone: This person is currently a member here? (Circle appropriate) Yes No	

CHILDREN (IF APPLICABLE)

Name:	Age	Contact

About your household (What would you like the church to know about your family)

_____

_____

_____

_____

_____	_____
Date	Signature

APPLICATION FOR CHURCH MEMBERSHIP FORM

PERSONAL INFORMATION

First name:	Middle:	Last:	Birthdate:

Address:	City:

State:	ZIP:	Email:

Phone:	Home phone:	Identity Number:

Tick Appropriate Box ☐ Single ☐ Married ☐ Divorced ☐ Widowed ☐ Separated ☐ Minor

Have you been baptized ? Yes ☐ No ☐ Baptism Date:	Baptism Location:

Have you been confirmed? Yes ☐ No ☐ Confirmation date:	Confirmation place:

Sex ☐ Male ☐ Female	Employer:

Work Address:	City:	State:	ZIP:

If student, Name of school:	City:	State:

Spouse/Parent's Name:	Employer:	Work Phone:

Emergency contact:	Phone:

PARENT/GUARDIAN/SPOUSE INFORMATION

Name:	Relationship:

Address:	City:	State:	Phone:

E-Mail:	Birthdate:	SSN:

Employer:	Address:

Work Phone:	This person is currently a member here? (Circle appropriate) Yes No

CHILDREN (IF APPLICABLE)

Name:	Age	Contact

About your household (What would you like the church to know about your family)

_____

_____

_____

_____

_____

_____	_____
Date	Signature

APPLICATION FOR CHURCH MEMBERSHIP FORM

PERSONAL INFORMATION

First name:	Middle:	Last:	Birthdate:

Address:	City:

State:	ZIP:	Email:

Phone:	Home phone:	Identity Number:

Tick Appropriate Box ☐ Single ☐ Married ☐ Divorced ☐ Widowed ☐ Separated ☐ Minor

Have you been baptized ? Yes ☐ No ☐ Baptism Date:	Baptism Location:

Have you been confirmed? Yes ☐ No ☐ Confirmation date:	Confirmation place:

Sex ☐ Male ☐ Female	Employer:

Work Address:	City:	State:	ZIP:

If student, Name of school:	City:	State:

Spouse/Parent's Name:	Employer:	Work Phone:

Emergency contact:	Phone:

PARENT/GUARDIAN/SPOUSE INFORMATION

Name:	Relationship:

Address:	City:	State:	Phone:

E-Mail:	Birthdate:	SSN:

Employer:	Address:

Work Phone:	This person is currently a member here? (Circle appropriate) Yes No

CHILDREN (IF APPLICABLE)

Name:	Age	Contact

About your household (What would you like the church to know about your family)

_____

_____

_____

_____

_____

Date	Signature

APPLICATION FOR CHURCH MEMBERSHIP FORM

PERSONAL INFORMATION

First name:	Middle:	Last:	Birthdate:

Address:	City:

State:	ZIP:	Email:

Phone:	Home phone:	Identity Number:

Tick Appropriate Box ☐ Single ☐ Married ☐ Divorced ☐ Widowed ☐ Separated ☐ Minor

Have you been baptized ? Yes ☐ No ☐ Baptism Date: Baptism Location:

Have you been confirmed? Yes ☐ No ☐ Confirmation date: Confirmation place:

Sex ☐ Male ☐ Female Employer:

Work Address:	City:	State:	ZIP:

If student, Name of school:	City:	State:

Spouse/Parent's Name:	Employer:	Work Phone:

Emergency contact:	Phone:

PARENT/GUARDIAN/SPOUSE INFORMATION

Name:	Relationship:

Address:	City:	State:	Phone:

E-Mail:	Birthdate:	SSN:

Employer:	Address:

Work Phone: This person is currently a member here? (Circle appropriate)   Yes   No

CHILDREN (IF APPLICABLE)

Name:	Age	Contact

About your household (What would you like the church to know about your family)

_____

_____

_____

_____

_____

_____   _____
Date   Signature

APPLICATION FOR CHURCH MEMBERSHIP FORM

PERSONAL INFORMATION

First name:	Middle:	Last:	Birthdate:

Address:	City:

State:	ZIP:	Email:

Phone:	Home phone:	Identity Number:

Tick Appropriate Box ☐ Single ☐ Married ☐ Divorced ☐ Widowed ☐ Separated ☐ Minor

Have you been baptized ? Yes ☐ No ☐	Baptism Date:	Baptism Location:

Have you been confirmed? Yes ☐ No ☐	Confirmation date:	Confirmation place:

Sex ☐ Male ☐ Female	Employer:

Work Address:	City:	State:	ZIP:

If student, Name of school:	City:	State:

Spouse/Parent's Name:	Employer:	Work Phone:

Emergency contact:	Phone:

PARENT/GUARDIAN/SPOUSE INFORMATION

Name:	Relationship:

Address:	City:	State:	Phone:

E-Mail:	Birthdate:	SSN:

Employer:	Address:

Work Phone:	This person is currently a member here? (Circle appropriate) Yes No

CHILDREN (IF APPLICABLE)

Name:	Age	Contact

About your household (What would you like the church to know about your family)

_____

_____

_____

_____

_____

_____	_____
Date	Signature

APPLICATION FOR CHURCH MEMBERSHIP FORM

PERSONAL INFORMATION

First name:	Middle:	Last:	Birthdate:

Address:	City:

State:	ZIP:	Email:

Phone:	Home phone:	Identity Number:

Tick Appropriate Box ☐ Single ☐ Married ☐ Divorced ☐ Widowed ☐ Separated ☐ Minor

Have you been baptized ? Yes ☐ No ☐	Baptism Date:	Baptism Location:

Have you been confirmed? Yes ☐ No ☐	Confirmation date:	Confirmation place:

Sex ☐ Male ☐ Female	Employer:

Work Address:	City:	State:	ZIP:

If student, Name of school:	City:	State:

Spouse/Parent's Name:	Employer:	Work Phone:

Emergency contact:	Phone:

PARENT/GUARDIAN/SPOUSE INFORMATION

Name:	Relationship:

Address:	City:	State:	Phone:

E-Mail:	Birthdate:	SSN:

Employer:	Address:

Work Phone:	This person is currently a member here? (Circle appropriate) Yes No

CHILDREN (IF APPLICABLE)

Name:	Age	Contact

About your household (What would you like the church to know about your family)

_____

_____

_____

_____

_____

_____   _____
Date   Signature

APPLICATION FOR CHURCH MEMBERSHIP FORM

PERSONAL INFORMATION

First name:	Middle:	Last:	Birthdate:

Address:	City:

State:	ZIP:	Email:

Phone:	Home phone:	Identity Number:

Tick Appropriate Box ☐ Single ☐ Married ☐ Divorced ☐ Widowed ☐ Separated ☐ Minor

Have you been baptized ? Yes ☐ No ☐	Baptism Date:	Baptism Location:

Have you been confirmed? Yes ☐ No ☐	Confirmation date:	Confirmation place:

Sex ☐ Male ☐ Female	Employer:

Work Address:	City:	State:	ZIP:

If student, Name of school:	City:	State:

Spouse/Parent's Name:	Employer:	Work Phone:

Emergency contact:	Phone:

PARENT/GUARDIAN/SPOUSE INFORMATION

Name:	Relationship:

Address:	City:	State:	Phone:

E-Mail:	Birthdate:	SSN:

Employer:	Address:

Work Phone:	This person is currently a member here? (Circle appropriate) Yes No

CHILDREN (IF APPLICABLE)

Name:	Age	Contact

About your household (What would you like the church to know about your family)

_____

_____

_____

_____

Date	Signature

APPLICATION FOR CHURCH MEMBERSHIP FORM

PERSONAL INFORMATION

First name:	Middle:	Last:	Birthdate:

Address: | City:

State: | ZIP: | Email:

Phone: | Home phone: | Identity Number:

Pick Appropriate Box ☐ Single ☐ Married ☐ Divorced ☐ Widowed ☐ Separated ☐ Minor

Have you been baptized ? Yes ☐ No ☐ Baptism Date: | Baptism Location:

Have you been confirmed? Yes ☐ No ☐ Confirmation date: | Confirmation place:

Sex ☐ Male ☐ Female | Employer:

Work Address: | City: | State: | ZIP:

If student, Name of school: | City: | State:

Spouse/Parent's Name: | Employer: | Work Phone:

Emergency contact: | Phone:

PARENT/GUARDIAN/SPOUSE INFORMATION

Name: | Relationship:

Address: | City: | State: | Phone:

E-Mail: | Birthdate: | SSN:

Employer: | Address:

Work Phone: | This person is currently a member here? (Circle appropriate) Yes   No

CHILDREN (IF APPLICABLE)

Name:	Age	Contact

About your household (What would you like the church to know about your family)

_____

_____

_____

_____

_____

_____

_____   _____
e   Signature

APPLICATION FOR CHURCH MEMBERSHIP FORM

PERSONAL INFORMATION

First name:	Middle:	Last:	Birthdate:

Address:	City:

State:	ZIP:	Email:

Phone:	Home phone:	Identity Number:

Tick Appropriate Box ☐ Single ☐ Married ☐ Divorced ☐ Widowed ☐ Separated ☐ Minor

Have you been baptized ? Yes ☐ No ☐	Baptism Date:	Baptism Location:

Have you been confirmed? Yes ☐ No ☐	Confirmation date:	Confirmation place:

Sex ☐ Male ☐ Female	Employer:

Work Address:	City:	State:	ZIP:

If student, Name of school:	City:	State:

Spouse/Parent's Name:	Employer:	Work Phone:

Emergency contact:	Phone:

PARENT/GUARDIAN/SPOUSE INFORMATION

Name:	Relationship:

Address:	City:	State:	Phone:

E-Mail:	Birthdate:	SSN:

Employer:	Address:

Work Phone:	This person is currently a member here? (Circle appropriate) Yes No

CHILDREN (IF APPLICABLE)

Name:	Age	Contact

About your household (What would you like the church to know about your family)

_____

_____

_____

_____

_____

_____   _____
te   Signature

APPLICATION FOR CHURCH MEMBERSHIP FORM

PERSONAL INFORMATION

st name:	Middle:	Last:	Birthdate:

dress:	City:

te:	ZIP:	Email:

one:	Home phone:	Identity Number:

k Appropriate Box ☐ Single ☐ Married ☐ Divorced ☐ Widowed ☐ Separated ☐ Minor

ve you been baptized ?   Yes ☐   No ☐   Baptism Date: Baptism Location:

ve you been confirmed?   Yes ☐   No ☐   Confirmation date: Confirmation place:

x ☐ Male ☐ Female   Employer:

ork Address:	City:	State:	ZIP:

tudent, Name of school:	City:	State:

ouse/Parent's Name:	Employer:	Work Phone:

ergency contact:	Phone:

PARENT/GUARDIAN/SPOUSE INFORMATION

me:	Relationship:

dress:	City:	State:	Phone:

Mail:	Birthdate:	SSN:

ployer:	Address:

ork Phone: This person is currently a member here? (Circle appropriate)   Yes   No

CHILDREN (IF APPLICABLE)

Name:	Age	Contact

About your household (What would you like the church to know about your family)

_____

_____

_____

_____

_____

_____	_____
e	Signature

Made in United States
Orlando, FL
12 February 2023

29935715R00070